Explore Space!

Space Missions

by Deborah A. Shearer

Consultant:
James Gerard
Aerospace Education Specialist
NASA Aerospace Education Services Program

Bridgestone Books
an imprint of Capstone Press
Mankato, Minnesota

Bridgestone Books are published by Capstone Press
151 Good Counsel Drive, P.O. Box 669, Mankato, Minnesota 56002
http://www.capstone-press.com

Library of Congress Cataloging-in-Publication Data
Shearer, Deborah A.
    Space missions / by Deborah A. Shearer.
    p. cm.—(Explore space!)
    Summary: Describes past space missions and explains the types of missions scientists
and astronauts perform during space travel, remotely by robot, and on the international
space station.
    Includes bibliographical references and index.   38888000014575
    ISBN 0-7368-1401-9 (hardcover)
    1. Astronautics—Juvenile literature. 2. Outer Space—Exploration—Juvenile literature.
[1. Astronautics. 2. Outer Space.] I. Title. II. Series.
TL793 .S429524 2003
629.4—dc21   2001008599

Editorial Credits
Christopher Harbo, editor; Karen Risch, product planning editor; Steve Christensen, series
    designer; Patrick D. Dentinger, book designer; Kelly Garvin, photo researcher

Photo Credits
All photos courtesy of NASA.

1 2 3 4 5 6 07 06 05 04 03 02

Table of Contents

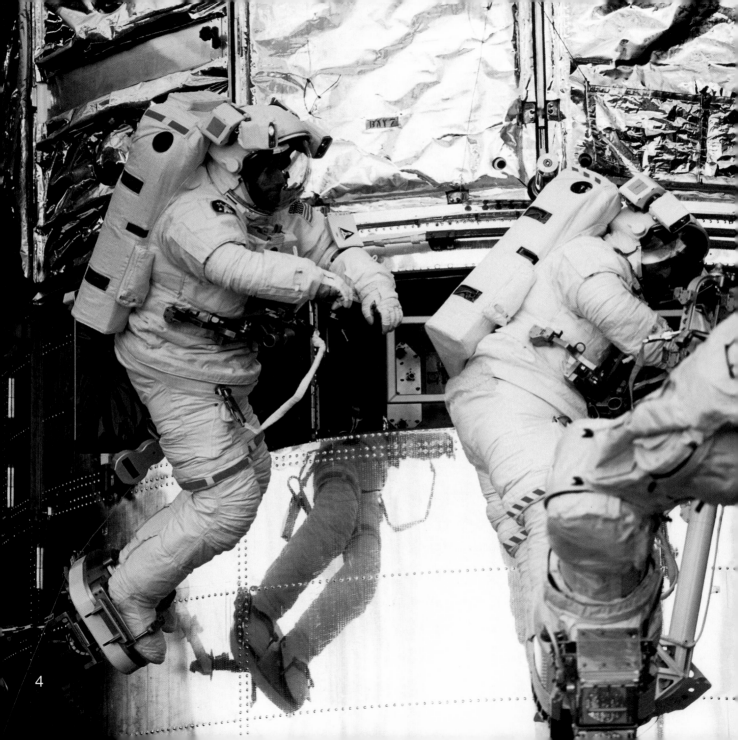

BAY 2

Space Missions

Scientists explore the solar system on space missions. A mission is a planned job or task. Space missions teach us about Earth, the Sun, and the planets. Space missions began in the late 1950s. Since then, machines, animals, and people have gone into space.

solar system
the Sun and the objects that move around it

5

6   Alan Shepard

First Missions in Space

The Soviet Union sent the first satellite into space. They also sent the first animal. In 1961, Russian Yuri Gagarin became the first person to travel into space. One month later, U.S. astronaut Alan Shepherd went into space. His flight lasted 15 minutes.

satellite
an object that circles Earth

7

Ed White

8

First Space Walks

In 1965, Alexei Leonov from Russia took the first space walk. Ten weeks later, astronaut Ed White from the United States walked in space. His space walk lasted 23 minutes. Today, astronauts walk in space to launch satellites and to repair spacecraft.

space walk
a period of activity spent outside a spacecraft by an astronaut

Neil Armstrong stepped on the Moon first. He said, "That's one small step for man, one giant leap for mankind."

The Moon Landings

The Apollo 11 spacecraft took the first U.S. astronauts to the Moon. On July 20, 1969, Neil Armstrong and Buzz Aldrin walked on the Moon. The United States made five more Moon landings after Apollo 11. These missions brought Moon rocks and soil back to Earth.

11

The International Space Station is the largest space station ever built.

The International Space Station

Astronauts use space missions to build the International Space Station. They live and work in the space station. Scientists use the station to study how people live in space. They also test new medicines on the space station.

medicine
a drug used to treat someone who is sick

13

**Viking 2 Lander
on Mars**

14

Missions to Mars

Scientists have sent many space probes to Mars. Viking 1 and 2 took pictures of Mars in 1976. Viking landers studied the soil on Mars. In 1997, Pathfinder brought a rover named Sojourner to Mars. Sojourner was like a remote-controlled car. It studied the rocks and soil on Mars.

probe
a tool or device used to study or explore something

15

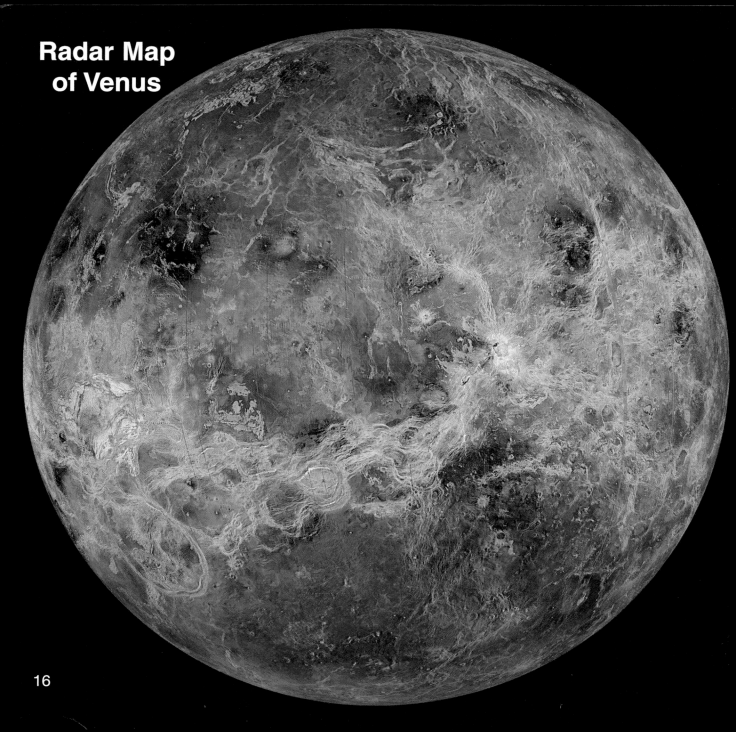

Radar Map
of Venus

16

Learning about Venus

Space missions have helped scientists learn more about Venus. Magellan began orbiting Venus in 1990. A thick atmosphere hides the surface of Venus. Magellan used radar to map the planet's surface. Magellan's radio waves went through Venus's atmosphere.

atmosphere
the mixture of gases that surrounds some planets

This NASA painting shows the Galileo spacecraft orbiting Jupiter. The blue dots stand for signals Galileo received from a smaller probe. Galileo sent the probe into Jupiter's clouds to study sunlight, temperatures, winds, and lightning.

Studying Jupiter

Scientists have sent six space probes to Jupiter. Voyager 1 flew by Jupiter in 1979. It discovered that Jupiter has rings of dust and ice. In 1995, the space probe Galileo studied Jupiter and its moons. It measured winds blowing 400 miles (640 kilometers) per hour on Jupiter.

20

Reaching the Outer Planets

Space missions teach us more about the solar system. Space probes have visited Saturn, Uranus, and Neptune. A space probe called Cassini will arrive at Saturn in 2004. Scientists built Cassini to study Saturn's largest moon and to travel through Saturn's rings.

Hands On: Mapping Venus

Venus's surface is hidden by a thick atmosphere. The Magellan space probe used radar to map Venus's surface. You can see how radar works.

What You Need

Clay	Aluminum foil
Aluminum pie pan	10 toothpicks

What You Do

1. Use clay to build mountains and valleys in the bottom of your pie pan. Be sure you make some low and some high spots. Keep your mountains below the top of the pie pan.
2. Cover the pie pan with aluminum foil. Pull the foil tight and pinch the edges around the pie pan. The foil is like the atmosphere around Venus. You cannot see the land below.
3. Gently push your toothpicks into the foil until you touch the clay below. Some toothpicks will stick up higher than others. The toothpicks act like radio waves. They show the high and low spots hidden under the foil.

Radio waves found the high and low spots under Venus's atmosphere. Magellan's radio waves traveled farther to reach valleys than to reach mountains. Scientists mapped Venus by measuring how far the radio waves traveled.

Words to Know

astronaut (ASS-truh-nawt)—someone trained to fly into space in a spacecraft

mission (MISH-uhn)—a planned job or task

orbit (OR-bit)—to travel around a planet or the Sun

probe (PROHB)—a tool or device used to study or explore something; space probes explore objects in outer space.

radar (RAY-dar)—a tool that finds solid objects by sending out radio waves; space probes use radar to map a planet's surface.

satellite (SAT-uh-lite)—an object that circles Earth; many satellites are machines that take pictures or send telephone calls and TV programs to Earth.

surface (SUR-fiss)—the top layer of something

Read More

Cole, Michael D. *International Space Station: A Space Mission.* Countdown to Space. Springfield, N.J.: Enslow, 1999.

Zelon, Helen. *Apollo 11 Mission: The First Man to Walk on the Moon.* Space Missions. New York: PowerKids Press, 2001.

Internet Sites

International Space Station
http://www.hq.nasa.gov/osf/funstuff/stationoverview/npage1.html

NASAKids
http://kids.msfc.nasa.gov

Index